YEALMPTON YESTERDAY

Peter Holloway

Fore Street in the early part of the century;
the town tree is in full leaf and all is peaceful.

This version of the book is virtually as originally published, presenting the work of Peter Holloway. There are now additional pages at the back providing information about the publisher, Arthur L Clamp.

The republishing project is being managed by Arthur's grandson, Steven Gibson. We aim to find all the research that he was involved in publishing, preserving it for the next generation as part of 'The Clamp Collection'.

INTRODUCTION

In the story of Yealmpton the earliest prehistoric remains are the extensive Kitley Caves which were inhabited by animals that included the hyena, cavelion and bear. The caves were discovered by quarrymen about 1800 and caves with even more remains were found at Yealmbridge but these, unfortunately, no longer remain as the area has been quarried.

The *Goreus Stone* still stands in the churchyard which is thought to be a memorial to an early British chieftain who had embraced Christianity. The Saxons gradually gained control of the area and nearly all the place names are Saxon. A legend that the Saxon king Ethelwold had a Palace in Yealmpton has no evidence to support it as history although there are a number of places which have been suggested as its site.

It is believed that Yealmpton was a Minster Church, a Mother Church of a large area as yet without smaller churches like the parish Church as we know it today. From this, plus the old Saxon font preserved in the church—for many years used as a flower pot in the vicarage—and the reference to clergy in the Domesday Book, we can only assume the existence of a pre-Norman Church building as there are no remains of a Saxon church. In A.D. 996, there were heavy raids by the Danes and again five years later and the village and church were probably sacked and burnt.

The Domesday Book shows that in Devonshire there were twelve Crown Lordships of which Yealmpton was one. When the Saxons conquered South Devon (A.D. 925) Athelstan gave away land of fair quality to Churches and nobles, but retained all the official centres and most bad land, which nobody wanted, as Crown property. Among these official centres was Yealmpton, referred to in Domesday Book as *Elintona* and in the Domesday entry a distinction is made between the property of the King and that of the Church.

King John gave the manor of Yealmpton to Matthew Fitz-Herbert, Lord of Stokenham, a soldier who was one of the barons at the making of Magna Carta. By marriage the manor passed to the Earls of Salisbury and in 1541 after the beheading on Tower Hill of a succeeding Countess of Salisbury, Henry VIII gave the manor as a dower to Queen Katherine Howard and then Queen Katherine Parr. In 1583 the manor was sold to John Hele of Wembury and from him it descended to his son, Sir John Hele, whose only daughter Jane was married to Sir Henry Hungerford of Farleigh Castle. The latter obtained power by Act of Parliament to sell his wife's property, and the manor was bought by John Pollexfen of Kitley in 1669. On the death of Edmund Pollexfen in 1710, his only surviving daughter Anne inherited the property and she, having been married to William Bastard of Gerston, whom she survived, brought the property into that family in whose hands it still remains.

Life in Yealmpton has always centred around farming and by Victorian times the village was virtually self-contained with all the shops and services that a community at that time could want. With the coming of the motor car and easy access to the large towns and cities, the small local shops and businesses could not survive and gradually dwindled away to the remaining few today. In its heyday, Yealmpton had an Annual Fair on 25th May. There was a cattle market during the fourth week of each month and Petty Sessions were held every third Monday in the Sessions House and Police Station, built in 1864 and now a private house. There was also a fire station and at varying times four public houses. In addition to the Church were a Wesleyan Chapel and two Plymouth Brethren Chapels. There were three cornmills and two National Schools, one erected in 1849 and the other in 1876. The former is now a private house and the other is still in use as the school today.

Yealmpton has grown considerably in the last few years with the addition of many houses. This book tries to give a glimpse of Yealmpton as it was in a selection of old photographs and pictures. My thanks are due to Miss Grace Yonge for letting me use the photographs taken by her father Rev. C. B. Yonge, to Mr. Tony Kingdom for lending me the railway items, Mr. Harry Pitts for the bus photograph, Kitley Estate for the bathing ticket and to Mr. Hedley Coleman and Mr. David Bramhall for some of the other items. Finally my thanks to Mr. Arthur L. Clamp who first suggested, and then made possible this book.

Peter Holloway,
Yealmpton, May, 1981.

THE PARISH CHURCH

The earliest mention of the Church occurs in a Charter of 1225. Nothing, however, of this building now remains. The present building was rebuilt between 1849-52 and at that time the old Church was in a bad state of repair. It was damp, the woodwork decayed and the doors were beyond repair. The floor was uneven and the vestry so dilapidated that the clergy could not use it. In the year 1846-47, the Church was re-roofed, but the old walls were too weak to bear the weight and rebuilding was absolutely necessary. The bulk of the cost, about £7,000, was borne by Edmund Pollexfen Bastard. The architect was William Butterfield, later an eminent Victorian church architect. At this time he was 35 years of age. Unfortunately, the building was never completed and it is not known how Butterfield intended the finished Church to look. However, John Betjeman has called it "the most amazing Victorian church in Devon". The exterior is not particularly outstanding, but inside are octagonal piers of local marble in two shades of grey. The chancel arch incorporates another arch slightly lower and the space between the two is filled with a multi-coloured diaper pattern. There is the bowl of a circular Norman font carved with wavy lines in low relief. From the old church there is a brass of Sir John Crocker, cup bearer to Edward IV, 1508.

Edmund Bastard died in 1856 and in 1860 the east window was inserted in token of the esteem in which he was held by the parishioners. In 1915 the tower was replaced as this had not been done during the rebuilding, but was found to be unsafe.

Rebuilding the Church tower in 1914.

The Rev. Warner is on the left and the *Goreus Stone* is in the foreground.

When the Church was restored in 1849 the only portion not rebuilt was the tower. In 1911 this was found to be unsafe and in 1912 work was started on repairing it. However, it was found to be beyond repair and in 1913 it was decided to have it completely rebuilt. Among the ideas for raising funds the Rev. H. J. Warner wrote a letter to children, in the local press, under the pen-name of *Old Mother Hubbard*. The letter was reprinted all over the world and the appeal brought in thousands of subscriptions. The tower was completed in 1915.

On the left is shown the cover of a booklet sold in aid of the Church tower fund.

The *Goreus Stone* from an engraving of 1808. It shows the stone lying on the north side of the churchyard. Its history is unknown but it is thought to be a memorial to an early British chieftain who had embraced Christianity and it is about 1400 years old. How long it had lain in this position is not known but it was moved to the present location near the tower in 1851.

On the night of February 26th and 27th, 1903, two great elm trees which stood on the west side of the churchyard fell on either side of the stone.

Several tombstones were smashed and the glass in the tower window broken but, although the stone was in the thick of the trees, it was absolutely unharmed.

Old Mother Hubbard's cottage in about 1910. Note the two new patches of thatch and the two horses detached from a cart presumably waiting for their owner to attach them to another cart or agricultural machine.

THE CHILDREN'S NURSERY RHYME

The nursery rhyme was written by Sarah Catherine Martin in 1805 when she was staying with her married sister at Kitley. The rhyme is supposed to have been based on the old housekeeper at Kitley at the time, although this was probably not her name. The story is also told that this housekeeper lived at the old cottage in Yealmpton known as Old Mother Hubbard's cottage. It is possible that she lived here after retirement but it is by no means certain. It is thought that the lines about the cupboard being bare relate to the great shortage of food at that time due to the Napoleonic wars.

Sarah Martin was the daughter of Sir Henry Martin, resident Commissioner of the Royal Navy at Portsmouth. A frequent visitor to her home was a young lieutenant serving in H.M.S. Hebe, who was Prince William Henry, third son of King George III and who would later become William IV. They fell deeply in love and both wanted to marry but it was tactfully suggested that it was Sarah's duty to her King to end the romance and this she did. Sarah went to London and the Prince was posted to the North American station. He continued to write to her father of his great love for his daughter. The Prince did not see her again and did not marry until he was 50 years of age. It is believed that Sarah did not marry and died in 1826, four years before the Prince became King.

The King had no children and if he had married Sarah and they had had children, then Queen Victoria would not have come to the throne and Old Mother Hubbard would never have been heard of. The original presentation copy of *The Comic Adventures of Old Mother Hubbard and Her dog*, is preserved in the library at Kitley.

The cover and illustration of a very early 'chapbook' of Old Mother Hubbard dated 1805.

Messrs. Tope, on the left, and Monk at Mother Hubbard's cottage around the turn of the century. How much would this early "horseless carriage" be worth today?

THE COMIC ADVENTURES OF OLD MOTHER HUBBARD AND HER DOG

Old Mother Hubbard
  Went to the Cupboard
To give the poor Dog a bone
  When she came there
  The Cupboard was bare
And so the poor Dog had none.

She went to the Baker's
  To buy him some bread
When she came back
  The Dog was dead.

She went to the Undertaker's
  To buy him a coffin
When she came back
  The Dog was laughing.

She took a clean dish
  To get him some tripe
When she came back
  He was smoking his pipe.

She went to the Alehouse
  To get him some beer
When she came back
  The Dog sat in a chair.

She went to the Tavern
  For White Wine and Red
When she came back
  The Dog stood on his head.

She went to the Hatter's
  To buy him a hat
When she came back
  He was feeding the Cat.

She went to the Barber's
  To buy him a wig
When she came back
  He was dancing a jig.

She went to the Fruiterer's
  To buy him some fruit
When she came back
  He was playing the flute.

She went to the Tailor's
  To buy him a coat
When she came back
  He was riding a Goat.

She went to the Cobbler's
  To buy him some shoes
When she came back
  He was reading the news.

She went to the semptress
  To buy him some linen
When she came back
  The Dog was spinning.

She went to the Hosier's
  To buy him some hose
When she came back
  He was drest in his clothes.

The Dame made a Courtsey
  The Dog made a Bow
The Dame said your Servant
  The Dog said Bow-Wow.

She went to the Garden
  To get him a Pippin
When she came back
  The Dog was skipping.

She went to the door
  To see who was ringing
When she came back
  She found him swinging.

She went to the Premier's
  To get him a place
When she came back
  He was playing the Bass.

She stept in next door
  To see Mrs. Riddle
When she came back
  He was playing the fiddle.

She went to the Market
  To buy him a Sheep's Head
When she came back
  He was sick in his bed.

She ran away quick
  To call Dr. Hulse
When she came back
  He was feeling his pulse.

She went to the Druggist's
  To get him a Pill
When she came back
  She found him at Drill.

He went out for a Bride
  That was handsome and show
As he came back
  He met with Miss Chloe.

She went out to Market
  In spite of the weather
When she came back
  They were dancing together.

She went to the kitchen
  To make him a mess
When she came back
  He was playing at chess.

She went to her neighbour's
  To see what was doing
When she came back
  She found him wooing.

She went to the Jeweller's
  To buy him a ring
When she came back
  They were learning to sing.

She went out to get him
  Some Fish to be fried
When she came back
  He presented his Bride.

The Bride made a Courtsey
  The Dog made a Bow
The Dame wished them joy
  They both said Bow-Wow.

This peaceful photograph of a lady sitting on the banks of the River Yealm was taken by the Rev. Yonge about 1900. It is from this river that Yealmpton takes its name and why a settlement came to be here at all. The river rises on Dartmoor and flows out to the sea near Wembury.

The *town tree* in full leaf overshadowing the nearby houses. Its fallen leaves in the autumn must have covered most of the highway.

This series of photographs shows Fore Street over a period of years at the beginning of the century. It also shows the big elm tree known as the *Town Tree* which stood here for nearly another fifty years. The houses on the left were all demolished during 1963. Apart from this the main thing which is different is the absence of any traffic. If the villagers of today stood around like their ancestors there would soon be a nasty accident!

The cottage in front of Elm Tree House on the right of the picture no longer remains. Note the surface of the main road.

The shop on the corner was Mrs. Perring's and the thatched one, a little further down, belonged to Mr. Daw the butcher. In between them was Mr. Alfie Percy, the village barber.

A view of Fore Street looking east. The building on the left with a person at its door was Vine's shop which was open until 1976.

Another view of Fore Street, slightly east of the centre view, in which can be seen the *Volunteer Inn* at the end on the left. Note some village children playing in the empty road.

Market Street in the early part of the century. The cottages on the right have been demolished and stood in front of the new houses in Elm Tree Close.

The large building on the left was formerly the Post Office, no longer standing, and the building on the right was the *Yealmpton Inn* now the *Rose and Crown*. This photograph was taken in 1910.

The buildings on the left of the picture have also been removed and the Yealmpton Health Centre has been built at their rear.

Speculation, a scene which has not changed a lot over the years. The main road leaving the village towards Plymouth is now well made up and certainly busier since this shot was taken.

Church Lane about 1920 when the photographer included these local people. Can anyone recognise them? On the 1913 O.S. map it is called the Borough. A name now revived in the new houses at Torr.

The cottages opposite the present entrance to Stray Park. The building in the centre was the village smithy. Trees appear to grow to great size in this area and were left to hang right over the roads as seen by this example.

An official G.W.R. photograph of the opening of the Yealmpton railway branch line which took place on 15th January, 1898. Note the broken tape falling in the picture and appearing blurred by the movement.

Ticket to the opening lunch.

This view shows Yealmpton station sometime between 1900 and 1910. The line had a chequered career and finally closed on the 29th February, 1960.

G.W.R. YEALMPTON

YEALMPTON BRANCH.

Down Trains.		Week Days only.							Up Trains.		Week Days only.						
		a.m.	a.m.	p.m.	p.m.	p.m.	p.m.	p.m			a.m.	a.m.	p.m.	p.m.	p.m.	p.m.	p.m
Plymouth {	Millbay ... dep	7 20	9 15	12 5	1 55	5 0	7 5	11 0	Yealmpton ...... dep	8 10	9 58	12 50	3 40	5 50	7 55	11 50
	North Road ,,	7 24	9 19	12 9	1 59	5 4	7 10	11 5	Steer Point ,,	8 17	10 4	12 56	3 48	5 57	8 3	...
	Mutley ... ,,	7 27	9 22	12 12	2 2	5 7	7 11	11 ?	Brixton Road ...... ,,	8 22	10 8	1 0	3 52	6 1	8 7	...
Plymstock ...... ,,		7 36	9 30	12 20	2 11	5 16	7 21	11 16	Elburton Cross ,,	8 26	10 13	1 5	3 57	6 6	8 12	...
Billacombe ...... ,,		7 40	9 33	12 23	2 15	5 20	7 25	11J21	Billacombe ...... ,,	8 29	10 16	1 8	4 0	6 9	8 15	...
Elburton Cross ,,		7 45	9 38	12 28	2 20	5 25	7 30	11J26	Plymstock ,,	8 34	10 20	1 13	4 5	6 14	8 20	...
Brixton Road ...... ,,		7 48	9 41	12 31	2 23	5 28	7 33	11J30	Plymouth { Mutley ... arr	8 43	10 28	1 21	4 13	6 22	8 28	12 24
Steer Point ...... ,,		7 52	9 45	12 35	2 27	5 32	7 37	11J35	{ North Road ,,	8 44	10 31	1 23	4 16	6 24	8 31	12 26
Yealmpton ...... arr		7 58	9 50	12 41	2 33	5 38	7 43	11 41	{ Millbay ,,	8 50	10 38	1 30	4 22	6 30	8 38	12 32

J—Calls to set down passengers only.

An official G.W.R. photograph of the opening of the Yealmpton railway branch line which took place on 15th January, 1898. Note the broken tape falling in the picture and appearing blurred by the movement.

The station just prior to the First World War with approaching staff and engine building up steam ready for its run back to Plymouth.

The Pollexfens resided at Kitley as early as the reign of Queen Elizabeth and Edmund Pollexfen, the last of the family, died in 1710. Ann, his heiress had married William Bastard of Gerston where that family had lived for many years and who were descended from Robert Bastard, who came to England with William the Conqueror. Kitley remains in the Bastard family today.

Kitley House, 1828.

It is believed that the original house was built in the reign of Henry VII (1457-1509) but the present house was re-modelled in 1820. The architect was G. S. Repton and the work was finished about 1825. The 18th century central staircase remains.

Kitley, 1830.

In the grounds of Kitley was quarried the only green marble found in England used in a number of important buildings. It was used for the staircase of the Natural History Museum in London, the columns in the nave of Brompton Oratory and the communion rails in the chapel of Welbeck Abbey.

Kitley House, 1906.

YEALMPTON, with the small hamlets of Dunston and Yealm Bridge, is a parish about seven miles from Plymouth, containing, including water area, 2,537 acres. Petty sessions are held monthly, and it has a cattle market, also held monthly. The church of St. Bartholomew has a square embattled tower and six bells. The living is a vicarage, with the perpetual curacy of Revelstoke annexed, worth £360 per annum. There are chapels for Roman Catholics and Methodists. There are National schools for boys and girls. There are reading rooms in the village.

POST-OFFICE.—Mr. Samuel Brock, sub-master. Arrival, 8.20 a.m.; letter box closes 4.20; despatch, 4.30 p.m. Money-orders granted and paid.

CARRIERS.—Plymouth, Chaffe, from house, Tuesday, Thursday, and Saturday, 9 a.m.; Jones, from house, Tuesday, Thursday, and Saturday, 9.30 a.m.

CLERGY, GENTRY, &c.

Anthony, Misses, Gloyen's park
Bastard, Baldwin J. P., Esq., Killey house
Bastard, Rev. Wm. P., Yealmpton villa
Bulteel, Miss, Yeo cottage
Eales, Rev. Wm. T. H., vicar, Vicarage
Ford, Mrs., Yeo
Harris, Captain William
Holberton, —, Yealm bridge
Mackay, John M., Paradise villa
Richards, Capt. R.N., Gloyen's park
Shannon, Mrs., Yealmbury villa
Shepherd, Mr. John, Weston
Shepherd, Mr. John, jun.
Strettle, Mrs., Yealmbury villa
Young, Mrs., Yealmbury villa

TRADERS, &c.

Adkins, Joshua Edward, surgeon, and medical officer to the Yealmpton District of the Plympton St. Mary Union
Anthony, John, miller, farmer, and corn manure merchants
Barratt, Amy, shopkeeper
Barratt, Thomas, miller and farmer, Yealm Bridge inn
Barratt, William, butcher and farmer
Blackler, James, saddle and harness maker
Brimblecombe, Charles, tailor
Brimblecombe, John, tailor
Brimblecombe, John, carpenter and joiner
Brock, Samuel, schoolmaster, newsagent, postmaster, and stationer
Brooks, Philip, farmer, Weston
Burford, John, Brewers' Arms
Cawse, Robert, tailor
Chaffe, John, carrier
Cornish, Charles, butcher
Cornish, John, shoemaker
Crocker, Richard, farmer, Wey
Davis, William, carpenter
Elliott, George, farmer, Treeby
Ford, Henry, farmer
Hall, Thomas, shoemaker
Hammick, shopkeeper
Horton, Grace, farmer, Orchard
Husband, Philip, shoemaker
Jenkins, Maria, farmer, East Pitten
Jenkins, William, shoemaker
Jones, William, carrier
Kerslake, Thos., victualler, Yealmpton Inn
Kelly, Thomas, solicitor, clerk to the magistrates and commissioners of taxes, and agent to the Royal Farmers' Insurance Company
Kingcombe, Andrew, painter and glazier
Lavers, Johanna, shopkeeper
Lavers, Richard, miller & farmer, Weston mill
Lavers, Robert, parish clerk
Lee, John, baker
Lidstone, Robert, shoemaker
Luke, J. and P., drapers and grocers
Luke, Philip, mason
Luke, Philip, jun.
Mann, Thomas, and Son, gig and car builders, and machine makers
Oldreive, Lewis John, land agent & surveyor
Patey, Elizabeth, milliner and dress maker
Pearce, Henry, registrar & relieving officer

Pearse, James, plumber and tinman
Radcliffe, John, shopkeeper
Robins, John, farmer and gamekeeper to Baldwin John P. Bastard, Esq., Stony Cross
Rogers, W. H., surgeon
Rudd, John, baker
Ryder, Abraham, victualler, Volunteer inn
Scoble, Robert, farmer, Efford
Shepherd, Charles, farmer, West Pitten
Shillabear, John, wood ranger
Shillibear, William, carpenter and coal dealer
Southwood, Wm., butcher and farmer
Snowdon and Co., bedstead and cabinet manufacturers, saw and turning mills, Yeard and Plymouth
Symonds, Joshua, blacksmith
Symons, John, blacksmith
Symons, Mrs., milliner and dressmaker
Symons, William, blacksmith
Tall, Geo., shoemaker, Tradesman's Arms
Tapley, Thomas, tailor, Lyneham
Tippett, William, tailor
Turner, Misses, dressmaker
Weeks, Thomas, tailor
Westcott, Jemima, and Cawse, M. A., grocers
Willcocks, John, farmer, Winsor

DUNSTON.

Adams, James, farmer
Dawe, Henry, farmer
Drake, Thomas, cooper and carpenter
Sherriff, Wm., timber dealer and builder
Giles, Joseph, manure agent, lime burner, collector of taxes, and agent to the Union Fire and Life Assurance office, Dunstan cottage

This entry for Yealmpton in White's Directory of 1862 gives an almost perfect record of the main people, trades and occupations which shows a very wide range of interests long gone.

Top right: The Rev. H. J. Warner and, *bottom right*, Mrs. H. Warner. Both photographs were taken in 1916. The Reverend Warner was vicar of Yealmpton from 1897 to 1917. He wrote the *History of Yealmpton*, now a rare book, and it was during his time in the village that the rebuilding of the Church tower took place.

The hamlet of Torr was formerly in the parish of Newton Ferrers until 1935 when it became part of the parish of Yealmpton. However, it often joined in celebrations with Yealmpton folk. The photograph on the left was taken in 1887 by Rev. Yonge.

This photograph was taken a few years later and a wall and gate have been put up. The Methodist chapel can be seen through the trees. Photograph also by Rev. Yonge.

This scene was taken in the 1920s and shows Torr Stores built on to the cottages shown in the previous two pictures. Torr Stores still remains but the cottage has gone.

Torr Bridge around the year 1900. The single span stone bridge crosses the river linking Yealmpton with Newton Ferrers.

Note the condition over the bridge of the unmade road surface. Most Devon roads and lanes were like this one and were difficult to travel on following rains.

Two more views of the old stone bridge. The tower of the parish Church can be seen in the background before it was replaced with the present structure in 1915.

An attractive scene at Torr Bridge with one local lady and five children posing next to the calm water of the Yealm. The cottage on the left stands where the Womens' Institute Hall is now. The cottage at the rear is still part of this local rural scene.

The village of Yealmpton as seen through a camera in 1918. The school is in the centre and the cottages at the crossroads have been replaced by a house.

Loading coal at Kitley Quay around 1886. Boats used to bring in various goods to the area as roads were not made to carry heavy vehicles. Carts then delivered the coal to farms and houses.

Below: Two sides of a pass issued by Kitley Estate for access to the pool at Kitley Quay.

KITLEY ESTATE.

BATHING PASS
SEASON 19

Name ....

(NOT TRANSFERABLE).

....

MANOR OFFICE,
YEALMPTON.

Issued 19

T.O.

Conditions on which this Pass is granted—

1.—Bathing Hours: 1 hour each side of high tide, on any day of the week.
2.—Bathing Drawers or Bathing Dress to be worn.
3.—Dressing and Undressing to be within the Screen provided for the purpose.
4.—Bathing to be from the Quay only.
5.—Entrance through Puslinch Bridge Lodge Gate only and along lower road south of Railway.
6.—No shouting, undue noise, or bad language allowed.
7.—This Pass to be shown to the Lodge Keeper.
8.—This Pass will be withdrawn if any breach of these regulations occur.

This cottage still stands although much altered. It is just past the entrance to Kitley Caves. Nowadays one can purchase ice cream and other items of refreshment here.

Puslinch House taken on 25th May, 1912.

Charlotte M. Yonge, a member of the family, was an emminent and prolific Victorian novelist and author. Her most famous novel was *The Heir of Redcliffe*. Miss Yonge often stayed at Puslinch. She is pictured here at Puslinch in 1886.

Puslinch is actually in the parish of Newton Ferrers but has always been closely connected with Yealmpton. The present house was built by James Yonge, the son of a Plymouth doctor, and finished in 1720. He had married Mary Upton in 1702, whose family had held the property for 230 years and had inherited it on the death of her father. The manor was held originally by Roger de Langford and later by the Mohuns before passing to the Uptons. The Yonge family still own Puslinch.

Puslinch Farm as seen in 1886. The Rev. Yonge took all the photographs on these two pages. He was vicar of Newton Ferrers at the turn of the century and an accomplished amateur photographer.

The ford below the clam on the river Yealm taken in 1886.

The clam, 1886. *Clam* is an old word for a single span bridge. This particular structure is now replaced with a newer one.

The old lime kilns below the clam in 1886. The entrance to Kitley Caves is on the right of the kilns. Lime burning was an essential part of the agricultural scene and there are still a number of these still in this area.

The Yealmpton Merryboys seen here in November, 1913. They were obviously enjoying themselves bedecked out with a variety of colourful clothes with faces suitably painted.

The Yealmpton Institute was the building now used as a showroom by Country Cottage Furniture. During the war this was also used by the American Forces as a recreation room.

The town band is here marching through the village on the occasion of the Coronation in 1937. Note the car in the foreground with bunting and a passing group of cyclists stopped by the town tree admiring the bandsmen and their music.

"Rockdale" and "Westpark" photographed by the Rev. Yonge in 1912 and still looking very much the same today as then. The new Wimpy houses have been built between them.

LYNEHAM

Lyneham gave name to a family who possessed the Manor till about the year 1340. In 1402 it belonged to John Crocker, son of John Crocker of Hele. Sir John Crocker who was born at Lyneham was held in great favour by King Edward IV and he was admitted to the office of cup bearer to the King and was knighted. He distinguished himself also on the part of Henry VII when he accompanied the Earl of Devon to the relief of Exeter when besieged by Perkin Warbeck in 1497. Sir John's son, another John, was high sheriff of the County of Devon in the reign of Henry VIII. Courtney Crocker, the last male heir, died in 1740. He left an only daughter who brought Lyneham to the Bulteel family. The house was rebuilt in 1699 and came into the possession of the Bastard family in 1838. The house has been extensively renovated in recent times.

Gnaton was the ancient seat of the Hele's and was considerably rebuilt about 1800 by Henry Roe. The wing on the right has now been demolished. Gnaton is now the home of the Hon. George Lopes, son of Lord Roborough.

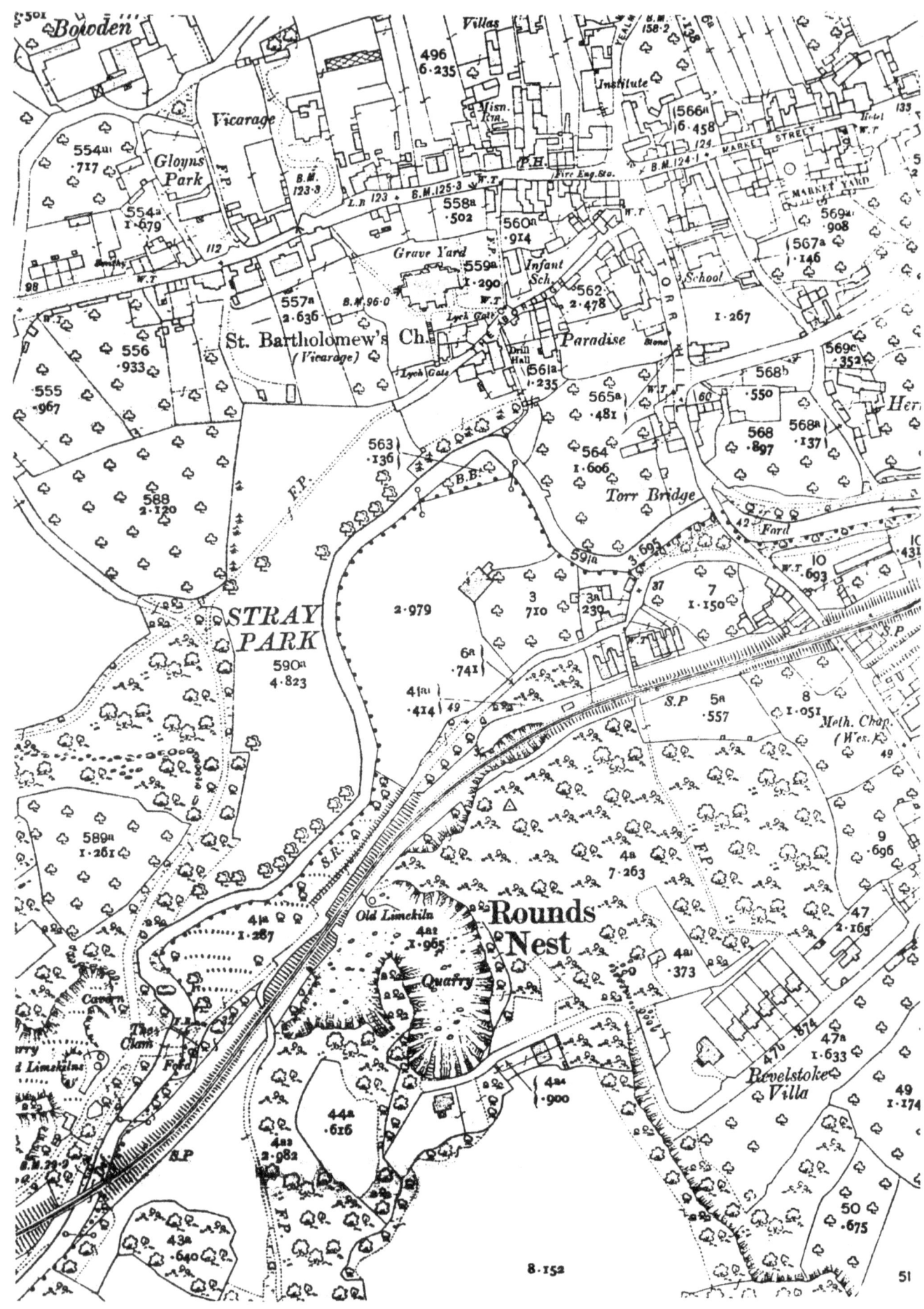

The ordnance survey map of Yealmpton in 1913.

Arthur L. Clamp – the man behind the books

Arthur Leslie Clamp was a man of boundless energy with a passion for helping others, particularly through his love of history. A printer by trade, he started his career in a printing company before moving his family from Exeter to Plymouth to teach at the Plymouth College of Art and Design, where he eventually became the Head of the Printing Department.

A Devoted Family Man

Arthur with his five children.

Despite his love of teaching, Arthur prioritised his family, always making it home by 5:30pm for tea. He and his wife, Rosemary, raised five children: Susan, Angela, Elizabeth, David, and Steven. Arthur would often combine his love of family and history by taking his children on Sunday walks, encouraging them to appreciate historical monuments by taking photos or making crayon rubbings of gravestones for his books. The family home at 203 Elburton Road was a hub of activity, with a large garden, featuring a two-storey fort and a makeshift swimming pool.

A Lifelong Learner and Adventurer

Arthur's thirst for knowledge extended beyond history to a deep curiosity about the world. He was passionate about exploring different cultures, traditions, and cuisines, often taking advantage of his long summer holidays as a teacher to travel to places like India, Russia, South America, the middle east and the USA, sometimes bringing one of his children along. This adventurous spirit even influenced his home life, as seen by the short-lived family tradition of steam-cooking vegetables after a trip to Iceland.

History is a prominent feature of family days out

Community and Philanthropic Spirit

His commitment to serving others was evident in his long-standing involvement with the Elburton Methodist Church. He was the Sunday School Superintendent for over 15 years and served as the editor of the wider church's monthly newsletter, "The Link," for a similar duration. After Rosemary's very sad passing, Arthur later remarried and, following a chance encounter with a professor from India, established a connection with a missionary school in Chennai. Together with his new wife, Christine, he co-founded a "Sponsor a Child's Education" program that continues to this day.

*Pictured left – The cover of 'The Link' complete
with hand drawn sketches of each church by Angela
Below right – Arthur Clamp promoting his latest book
Below left – Arthur at home with his first wife, Rosemary
Below centre – Arthur on holiday with his second wife,
Christine*

A Legacy of Learning and Positivity

Arthur's greatest passion was history, which he brought to life through tireless research, documentation, and the many books he authored. He was driven by a need to "never be stuck in a rut," constantly seeking new experiences, meeting new people, and expanding his knowledge. With a positive attitude and a great sense of humour, he was always ready to help others, leaving a lasting impact on his family and community. His children, Susan, Angela, Elizabeth, David, and Steven, remember him with love and gratitude.

David Clamp, 2025

A Legacy of Local History

Below is the story of how Arthur L Clamp began writing books, in his own words, drafted shortly before he passed away in 2001. I have only made minor alterations to this text, correcting grammatical errors that he did not survive to correct himself. When I first discovered this text, I was shocked to see my name mentioned. It seems that, unbeknownst to me, I shared my first PC with him. I suspect he used it during the day when I was at school, although I do have one memory of sitting with him and showing him how it worked. It has been a pleasure to pick up where he left off and see his books republished and redistributed, and to know that I was part of the story, even back then. It was also fascinating to discover that his pricing structure matches the way I have tried to price the books, with a third going to local sellers and the rest covering printing costs with a little left over for my expenses.

I am his eldest grandson, and it is a privilege to curate his legacy, which we are calling 'The Clamp Collection'. The very last line of the text originally reads "The following pages list all the titles." Sadly, that page is missing and we have no record of all the books he published and knowing that some of those were researched by other authors makes the process of finding them even harder. I look forward to one day completing the collection and seeing them all available again. And maybe, one day, I'll even start writing my own to add to the series. For now, here is his story in his own words.

Steven Gibson, 2025

Writing and Publishing Booklets on Local Topics and Areas

I started this interest in either 1968 or 1969 when living in Woodford. I had by these dates established the Department of Printing and I think I must have been looking for something different to do. The first titles were of A5 size proofed from type set at Clarke, Doble and Brendon, Ltd., Plymouth printers, and then made up into pages and printed at Sawtell and Neilson, Ltd., Totnes.

Then began a slow process of getting them out to shops, etc. which proved to be more time consuming and difficult than actually researching, writing and getting the books into print. However, I persisted and opened a business account with Barclays Bank on the Broadway. I was advised to give it a title so I called it "Westway Publications". There came along another problem, one of storage of paper and finished books which was solved when the family moved to Elburton in 1970.

I changed the printer to Penwell, Ltd., Callington, Cornwall, as he was then just setting up himself and his prices seemed very reasonable. I did not get any of the printers to make up the complete books. I hand folded the flat printed sheets, stitched the books on a small manual table stitcher and trimmed them in a small hand turned guillotine which I bought from someone in Penzance for £40. It was brought up in a van.

The trouble and time going to and fro to Callington was too much so I transferred the printing to PDS Printers, Prince Rock, Plymouth, and I have been with them ever since. Now they are at Plympton which is easy to reach and they fold the flat sheets which was turning out to be a long chore which only saved a small part of the printing costs.

All my first titles were written by myself. I took the photographs and developed them in the loft of the house, the type was set by now on a computer situated in the house at Elburton from which I had collected photographic lengths of text to cut up and law down as pages.

At some point I decided that I would do my own film processing of lith film so I bought a large second hand process camera from Kingsbridge and learnt through trial and error to make line negatives of the text and halftone negatives of the illustrations which proved more difficult than I anticipated. The main problem was trying to keep the developer in the large dish at the correct temperature as any change would affect the developing time. I replaced this old camera with a brand new one bought from Croydon, Surrey, costing £900. This has turned out to be a great asset cutting out an expensive part of the printer's costs and one crucial aspect of the work which I could control.

By the middle 1970s there were many outlets I had contacted in Plymouth, up to Dartmoor, Exeter, around to Torbay, Totnes, Dartmouth and the South Hams. The market for local books was much greater than I had first thought and through getting to know many local people undertaking research themselves had the chance to help and make up books for other people who had in most instances, got together a collection of photographs with some text in a rather muddled way. Through my experience in print I was able to shape up their work and get it into print and in every case I had to pay the printer and let the person have the royalties. In the majority of titles produced in this manner this was another way of producing titles and it did give some profit to my work. However, I must say that in a few cases I lost out by either the other person getting the numbers wrong, not returning any monies from stock I delivered or they thought that more of their books should have been sold.

The print run was usually 1,000 copies and from time to time I have had reprints of 250 copies. It took about ten years to clear the first print run so I always had large stocks in the garage, workshop, etc. The numbers sold during the early years was about 7,000 copies a year increasing to around 9,000 copies and for the whole of the enterprise about 500,000 have been sold. The booklets have become part of the local scene and many people collect them, shops regularly order copies and I go around certain areas month by month restocking or replacing titles as necessary.

During the past year or so I have started setting the text on a Packard Bell PC, something which I should have done some years back. I share it with Steven Gibson, my grandson. There appears to be no end to the market for local books, but I could not earn a regular income because of the long time it takes to sell stock.

However, now exceeding 100 titles made up mainly of A4 twenty-four page booklets, some folded guides, with selling prices set with a third going to the shop which is the trade custom, the original idea has been quite successful and could go on for ever.

Apart from monetary benefits, however spasmodically these might be, I have learnt a lot myself, met many interesting people and have become part of the local scene with requests to give talks and to advise people about getting into print.

Arthur L Clamp, 2001

This newspaper article, published by the Evening Herald on 17th August 2001, forms a good record of his life. Just as he encourages us to learn more about local history, we encourage you to learn a little about him. For that reason, we have included these pages at the back of all the most recently republished books, in honour of his memory and recognition of his contribution to the community.

www.ingramcontent.com/pod-product-compliance
Lightning Source LLC
Chambersburg PA
CBHW061409070526
44584CB00031B/4194